Nursery School Bulletin Boards

Extending the Learning Environment

CLARE CHERRY

DIRECTOR
Congregation Emanu El
Experimental Nursery School and Kindergarten
San Bernardino, California

Photography by SAMUEL A. CHERRY

Fearon Teacher Aids
Carthage, Illinois

ISBN-0-8224-4786-X   Printed in the United States of America.

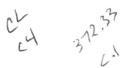

Preface

When I enter a classroom, I want to focus on the children and what they are doing—not on the teacher's artistic or decorative talents or lack of same. The purpose of this handbook is to present easy-to-use suggestions for an approach to bulletin boards as an integral part of the child's activities. They are meant to complement, not replace, three dimensional learning centers and classroom experiences. The examples are typical of those which might be used during one school year. They combine the natural interests of the child with teacher-initiated learning opportunities. I did not include patterns because of my strong belief in the superiority of one's own imagination over artistic talent. I have attempted to keep the selections simple. If you feel that any of the projects are beyond your capabilities, take the opportunity to utilize the services of one or more of your children's parents by asking them to help you. They will appreciate being seriously involved in your program. However you make use of this book, I sincerely hope it will inspire you to take a fresh view of your classroom, motivate a new boldness in using space and materials in your own way, and create a willingness to leave plenty of unused space for the child's own flowering imagination.

The bulletin boards presented in this book were created with the assistance of present or former members of the staff of Congregation Emanu El Experimental Nursery School and Kindergarten. For their research, interest, and inspiration, I especially want to thank Lael Cohen, Barbie Gaines, Bettye Kovitz, Janet Peters, Alyce Smothers, Barbara Stangl, Halliette Stubbs, and Helen (Sunny) Wallick. I wish to take this opportunity to express my sincere appreciation to them for their cooperation and patience with me as I began to view their bulletin board displays with a critical eye while considering which ones to include in this book. I also wish to give my thanks to the many parents who assisted in the classrooms, to Auri Ohna for helping with the drawings, and to my friends and members of my family whose encouragement and continuous help played so important a role in completing this project.

Clare Cherry

Contents

Bulletin Boards in the Classroom

Look around your classroom—particularly at your bulletin board displays. Are they stereotyped, static, dull? Did you find that preparing them was a tedious chore? Did you finally put up just anything as long as it took up lots and lots of space? If you answered yes to these questions, chances are that your bulletin boards are taking up valuable space that could be put to more profitable use. The bulletin board should be a vital part of your classroom environment—not just a decoration It should be considered as an extension of the learning environment and a focus for continuing class discussions and activities. In addition, it can be used to motivate the child to think critically and creatively, involve his senses, and introduce new concepts. Remember, the purpose of the bulletin board is *not* to decorate the walls or impress parents and your fellow staff members. If it is decorative and impressive, that's fine—but its main purpose is to serve the child.

The well-planned classroom has many areas of interest. Your bulletin boards should complement and supplement these centers, not dominate the classroom. One way to avoid overemphasizing your bulletin boards is to design each display for close-up, rather than long-distance, viewing. To design them effectively, approach the problem from the child's point of view. One very basic consideration is height. A child's eyes are approximately thirty to forty inches from the floor, while yours are between fifty-five and sixty-five inches above it. What is comfortable for you to see is going to be about two feet too high for the child. To get the right height for the child, try setting up your bulletin boards from a kneeling position.

The best, most complete learning takes place through total sensory involvement, yet the child is constantly being told to keep his hands off things. The curriculum for the young child, and the bulletin boards that introduce and reinforce it, should be riots of sensory experiences. He should touch, smell, and even taste when appropriate. If you hear yourself saying, "Hands off! Don't touch," then it's time to reevaluate what you are doing. Remember that the board is a teaching tool, and that for the child to learn, all five senses must be involved whenever possible. To deprive him of touching is to leave much of the learning experience incomplete.

- Bulletin boards are especially suited to touching and feeling. Whenever possible, incorporate textures and shapes into your displays (consistent and not in conflict with the points to be taught).

- Prepare small displays and place them where they can be "discovered" by the children.

- Prepare a touching board with various textured materials; rough, smooth, spongy, sticky, bumpy, or slick.

- Make a display of textured materials and have children match photographs or illustrations to the displayed items.

- Put objects inside paper bags and have pupils identify them by touch only. Have a touching corner with displays and boxes containing objects of widely differing textures for pupils to handle and explore.

Some Basic Principles

PLANNING

- Select an appropriate theme according to the time of the year, the curriculum, interest of the child, or a special event or activity.

- Block out a master plan for your display. Often rummaging through your resource materials will stimulate new ideas. Look at store displays, window decorations, billboards, and space ads with an eye to borrowing design elements.

- Make several sketches to plan the design. Simple arrangements and mountings are best for young children.

- Select materials for creating your display. Think in terms of shape, texture, and other visual and tactile elements. Don't forget color.

- Allow for as much involvement as possible on the part of children. Remember, your bulletin boards are for teaching, not decoration.

- Build your display, then watch carefully as children interact with it. Revise the content or rearrange the elements if your observations tell you that the board could be more effective.

- Supplement your own drawings with pictures from magazines, catalogs, and old storybooks. Don't be afraid to make your own drawings. Keep them childlike, and you won't go wrong.

DESIGN

Throughout the planning and execution of your bulletin boards, keep these basic principles in mind:

Color

- Remember that a color is affected by other nearby colors. For example, in a picture with a yellow sun and blue sky, if you use a yellow green foreground, the sun will not look as bright as it would if the foreground were blue green, because the yellow in the foreground will absorb some of the yellow from the sun.

- Experiment with color combinations. Cut a disc from colored paper and place it on different backgrounds. Note which color combinations are most pleasing and what "moods" they create.

Composition

Studies show that pictures are usually viewed from the bottom to the top, then the viewer focuses most readily on the center or slightly to the right and above of center. No matter what the subject, try to place something of interest in the general area of focus, even if your main theme is carried out elsewhere.

Balance

Balance can be attained through several arrangements.

Symmetric • This is formal balance in which the two sides are evenly spaced and colors are balanced. The main area of interest is in the exact center.

Asymmetric • Balance is achieved by counterbalancing elements (sizes, shapes, colors). In this illustration the main theme is low in the center. Color arrangement and placement of other items in the picture help bring the eye into focus and unite all parts of the picture.

Symmetric

Asymmetric

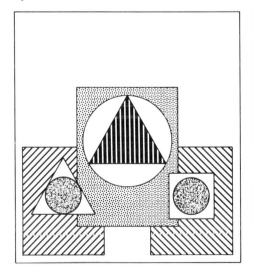
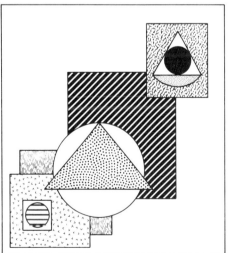

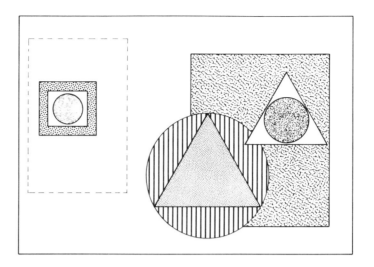

The isolated figure on the left counterbalances the large grouping on the right. The weight of the small picture is enhanced by the pressure of the surrounding mass of clear space. The addition of a large mat behind the small picture would have cut into the effectiveness of the display.

Background

Backgrounds are important to the overall design. They should be given as much consideration as the foreground. Avoid the temptation to cover the background space. Blank or negative space can play an effective part in composition.

- Sketch your design to show negative space as shown in these illustrations.

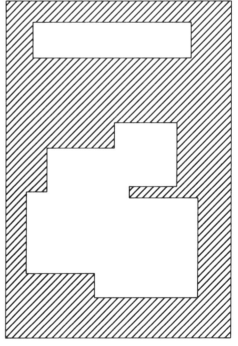

Color and texture actually become part of the subject matter and are not part of negative space, but are actually part of the main design. Their use, while helping to create balance in a picture, should be tailored to the subject.

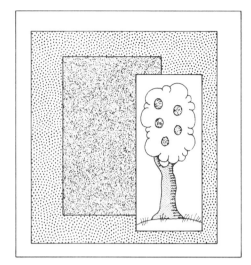

In this illustration of an apple tree, a deep red paper mat placed over tan paper is utilized to balance the narrow picture. The red repeats the color of the apples and the tan harmonizes with the dark brown tree trunk.

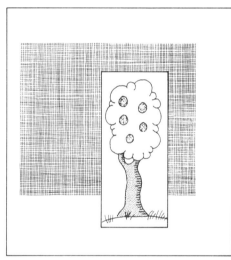

Here the same apple tree is balanced by a deep green, loosely woven grass mat that harmonizes with the green leaves of the tree and blades of grass. The grass mat is in keeping with the subject and would have been out of place in, for example, a sea scene.

Color Planning

An elementary knowledge of basic color principles will help you plan better displays. Post a simplified color chart that can be easily copied and colored with crayons on a staff bulletin board for reference.

- *Primary Colors.* Red, blue, yellow.

- *Secondary Colors.* Orange, violet, green.

- *Intermediate.* Made by mixing any primary color with an adjacent secondary color.

- *Complementary.* Colors directly opposite one another on the chart (orange and blue; red violet and yellow green)

- *Split Complements.* Select a pair of complements. Then, use the two adjacent colors in place of *one* pair (red/yellow green and blue green). Use one set of complements at time. Two sets will wipe one another out—you're using almost the entire color wheel. Complements can be softened or intensified by adding white or black to the basic colors, depending on the mood you wish to create.

- *Adjacent Colors.* Any two or three colors which are adjacent to one another on the chart will go well together.

- *Single Color.* Two or more shades or tints of a single color are easy to handle. Single color arrangements are especially effective if accented with black and/or white.

- *Black and White.* These colors can be added to any arrangement without upsetting the color scheme.

- *Realistic Colors.* Although colors do not have to be realistic to be effective, aesthetic considerations are important. For example, eyes might be colored green to create a specific tone, but pink or orange eyes would be offensive to most viewers.

Arranging Mountings

Keep mountings simple. Staggered arrangements, fancy curves, zigzags, and other intriguing designs are good for older children and adults, but are likely to confuse young children. A little practice will help you learn how to use mats or mountings effectively to unify displays, or create a visually pleasing arrangement of shapes or colors that might in themselves clash. Overlapping is an effective way of making connections between elements of a display.

Alternative Bulletin Boards

- If your bulletin boards aren't satisfactory—if they're poorly placed, too far off the floor, insufficient in number—don't give up on using bulletin board displays. Here are some typical problems and solutions.

- Combination chalkboard and corkboard wall panels are usually too high for most small children. Use the lower portion only and/or cover the space beneath the chalk tray with corrugated cardboard. Children work very effectively at this level—they can spread out whatever they are working with and sit next to it on the floor.

- If the bulletin board is too high, use it as a support for lower displays. Suspend displays from it, attach corrugated paper to it and let the paper hang to a workable level.

- If the bulletin board is shared with other groups, such as Sunday School classes, leave the permanent display intact and cover it with your own portable fold-up or roll-up displays during the week.

- If the entire wall is covered with a floor-to-ceiling display surface, rejoice. But keep the children in mind and do not place any display higher than four feet above the floor. And be sure to leave plenty of empty space between separate displays.

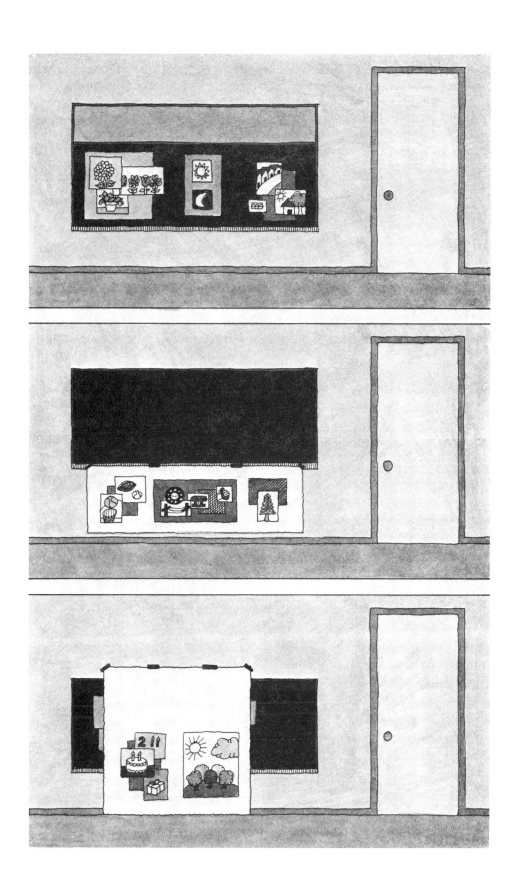

One long, continuous bulletin board has to be used for several displays, often unrelated. Use devices to separate areas of focus so that no confusion or mental overlapping takes place with the children. This type of situation poses a real challenge since, in order to keep the displays from clashing, color planning will be essential. Colors must harmonize without creating a false sense of continuity from display to display. Texture and shape will play important roles in defining the different displays.

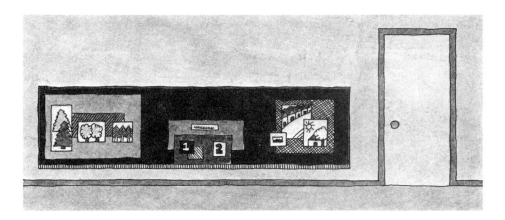

There just isn't any wall space available. The room has to have a few doors and probably some storage cabinets with doors. The piano can be placed so that its back can be covered with an appropriate bulletin board surface. Portable stands may be constructed as combination room dividers and bulletin boards. Folding screens make good dividers and display areas. These simple-to-make screens are empty window frames purchased from a lumber yard and hinged together. Chart racks (home-made or commercial) make good display areas. Even a tilted chair can be used as a temporary support for portable displays.

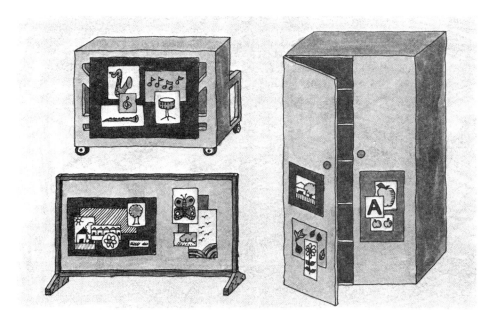

The bulletin boards hang over built-in storage cabinets or are otherwise out of the child's reach. Forget them. Make them decorative or use them for parent notices, but forget them as teaching aids. Use portable displays instead.

Windows, windows, everywhere, and not a bulletin board in sight. Use the space beneath, as with the chalkboard. Consider using some of the window shades. If the windows extend from floor to ceiling, then fit cardboard panels into some of the casements.

Making Portable
Bulletin Boards

Basically any material in which a pin can be inserted and which will hold some weight on that pin can be used for portable bulletin boards.

- A piece of cardboard may be made into a stand-up board by the addition of a stiff cardboard support. The same cardboard section can be hung from a wire or string inserted through punched holes.

- Two pieces of equal-sized cardboard can be hinged together with cloth or plastic tape.

- Several pieces of cardboard can be hinged together to form an accordian-style, free-standing display board.

- Plywood panels can be converted into bulletin boards by covering them with good display cloth such as felt, burlap, or flannel. The cloth should be cut approximately 2″ larger than the base on which it is to be mounted. Cutting the corners on a diagonal will allow mitering of the corners. The best means of fastening the cloth to the board would be a heavy-duty staple gun, but it could also be glued or fastened with masking tape.

- An artist's table easel is an excellent support for portable displays. Watch garage sales and junk shops for these items.

- If your budget is really tight and your facilities less than workable, brown wrapping or butcher paper can be used to create workable display areas. This arrangement has its limitations, but it does provide a display area when needed.

- Cork panels are now readily available at most decorating supply houses, hardware and lumber companies, and discount houses. Most of these are very messy—they shed large amounts of coarse, brown dust, but this can be eliminated for a time by spraying the surface with a clear plastic coating. The edges of these boards tend to chip easily and it is better to frame them before using them unless you intend to attach them right to a wall. Even then, there may be a temptation for some children to pick away at the edges.

- Fiberboard (brand names like Celotex) is an inexpensive wall paneling material that provides an excellent bulletin board surface. It can be purchased at almost any lumber company. It is quite sturdy, but framing is recommended to keep the edges from chipping and shredding.

- Corrugated cardboard packing carton panels are about as inexpensive and effective a surface as you can find.

- If you want to paint any of your portable or permanent boards, use a flat latex wall paint. It is fast drying, washable, and comes in a variety of attractive colors. A substitute can be made by mixing canned milk with tempera paint. The milk dries to a hard finish and will prevent the color from rubbing off.

- Some of your displays will be most effectively and efficiently prepared if they are permanently attached to posterboard so they can be stored and reused at intervals. These types of boards are versatile and can be pinned to existing display surfaces, set on easels or chalk trays.

- You can purchase large rolls of corrugated paper for bulletin board use. It comes in a variety of colors, is relatively inexpensive, and is quite durable.

- Styrofoam panels make good emergency portable bulletin boards. They are not, however, very good for children to hang things on because the surface is too porous. To make displays "stick," you'll need long pins inserted at an angle.

Bulletin Board Projects

NAMES

The Name Tag Tree (September 10)

Everyone has a name, and it's hanging on the name tag tree. Capitalize on opportunities to write each child's name. Most children who have learned to recognize their names before coming to school have learned capital letter forms. You may wish to continue using capitals for a time, then add lower case letters gradually. Children can become familiar with both types simultaneously if given plenty of time.

- Use scraps of brown corrugated paper to form the trunk and branches. Emphasize the texture with lines from a black felt-tip pen. Cut leaves from construction paper in varying shades of green. The child who is just learning to recognize his name can use the shade as an additional clue. Add simple cutouts of boys and girls and a few flowers for interest and color.
- If the tree does not appeal to you, or if you want a change of scenery, try a flower petal display. Sometimes the entire flower is planted in a pot and then transplanted in the garden when the child arrives at school. The flowers are made of construction paper with black broom-straws for stems.

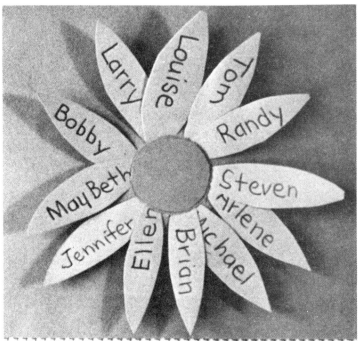

Clap the rhythm of each child's name as part of your music program.

- Make up a story using a child's name, and encourage that child to elaborate on the story. More than one child's name can be included in a story. Substitute each child's name in traditional stories and songs.

- Play "Names." The child who is "it" calls each child by name. If he forgets a name or calls a child by the wrong name, he relinquishes his place to the child who stumped him.

Sweaters and Autumn Leaves (October 1)

It's time to note the change of seasons. Encourage the child to bring interesting leaves to school and hang them on the tree. Let each child pick his favorite leaf to replace his name tag on the cardboard tree.

- After a long hot summer, it's hard to remember sweaters. Wooly pieces of cloth (traced from a pattern cut to fit a paper doll's torso) make nice sweaters for the bulletin board children. Attach them with rubber cement.

Autumn Winds (October 15)

- A squirrel scurries up a tree with another nut for his winter store. Have the pupils move the leaves from the branches to the ground, just a few each day.

- Time to add winter clothes. Corduroy was my choice because it has such a nice texture and is heavy and warm to the touch.

- The squirrel is made of pellon (excellent for later use on a flannel board) and the nuts are real.

Related Activities This display can be used to reinforce many learning experiences. How many leaves are still on the lowest branch? The highest? How many yellow leaves do you see? Red? Brown? Find the biggest branch and the smallest branch.

Winter Is Coming (November 1)

- The leaves have all fallen and it's time to clean up the yard and prepare for winter. Actual items of clothing can be used to form the new figure. Cut paper hands and a face to complete the body.

- By now the child has collected leaves, felt their textures, smelled them, crushed them, and manipulate them on bulletin board displays. Cut out a variety of tissue paper leaves. Let the children use liquid starch to paste the leaves onto the butcher paper, which is then added to the display.

- The girl in the swing was cut from a magazine and attached to the tree branch with a loop of black yarn.

  Related Activities Cut giant leaf shapes out of newspaper. Let each child paint his leaf with a variety of fall colors.

- The child can make rubbings of his favorite leaves by placing a leaf on a table with the back side (veins) facing up. Place drawing paper over the leaf, peel the paper from a crayon stub, and rub over the leaf with the side of a crayon. Finished rubbings can be cut out and pinned or pasted to large bulletin board displays.

Snow on the Ground (December)

Styrofoam panels can be cut and shaped to give the appearance and texture (minus the cold) of real snow. You can even glue strips of cotton to the branches. Here, the children decorated teacher-made paper snowflakes using scraps of turquoise and magenta tissue paper.

Through the Year

The cardboard tree can be continued through the year. Modify the snow scene with a house in the background, fir trees, and so on. A bird in the tree and a squirrel family herald the arrival of spring. Green and ripening fruit is added at the appropriate time, and for interest, children and pets might picnic or play beneath the tree.

Black and green pipe cleaners can be used to form trees. Cotton balls dyed with paints or food coloring can be added as blossoms or fruit. Scenery for dramatic play is constructed using large cardboard cartons, flattened and painted with a blue sky, green grass, and other background items. Trees, houses, flowers, and other appropriate items can then be made from paper or painted on the backdrop.

Seasonal Clothing

Subjects introduced by one bulletin board display should be reinforced by other displays. The seasonal theme can be picked up as an activity on appropriate dress for different types of weather. Give the child simple cutouts of body shapes along with a wide variety of material scraps. The child can then dress the paper dolls collage-style with the scraps. The older child may wish to create his own dolls to dress.

- Once each child has dressed his cutout, provide a summer/winter bulletin board and have him pin it to the appropriate display.

  Related Activities A variety of indoor/outdoor classification activities can be carried out with this same two-panel board: toys that are used indoors and outdoors, for example, or animals that might be found inside a child's home and those that would be found only outdoors.

- The indoor/outdoor theme offers many opportunities for creative play and role playing, art activities, songs, and dance. In initiating oral language development, capitalize on the child's experience.

ADDRESSES

Everyone lives in a house. It may be a single residence, a mobile home, or a high-rise apartment complex, but the child will call it "my house." Take pupils for a walk through the neighborhood and observe the different types of dwellings. Discuss features like doors, windows, roofs, chimneys, and colors. Then have the child cut pictures from magazines and make a display of houses. This activity can be expanded to show houses from different parts of the world.

Animals Live in Houses Too

Collect pictures of animal houses (dog house, bird cage, fox den) and discuss how animal families live inside shelters. Explore the necessity of shelter for animals (protection from weather, safety for young). Read and dramatize "The Three Little Pigs." Why did the straw house blow down so easily? Why did the brick house remain standing?

Every House Has An Address

Take a walk and look for numbers on houses. Go past the house of a child who lives nearby. Personalize the lesson by showing the class the child's house number and street name. Tell them to look for their own when they go home.

- Send a letter to parents explaining that the class is learning about addresses. Ask each parent to send an envelope to school with his child. If possible, obtain photographs of each child's house showing the house number. Enlist the help of parents in teaching children their addresses.

- Post the pictures and envelopes on a bulletin board, then add a picture or cutout of a green parrot. Teach pupils the following rhyme:

> The little green parrot likes to repeat
> The number of my house and the name of my street.

- Vary the display by cutting a large house out of construction or art paper. Arrange the envelopes and pictures in attractive groups. Attach them with small dabs of rubber cement so the display can be changed or rearranged with ease.

Learning Your Own Address

Make another, smaller, house of construction paper and introduce it by noting that it has no address. Ask children if they will let the house "borrow" their

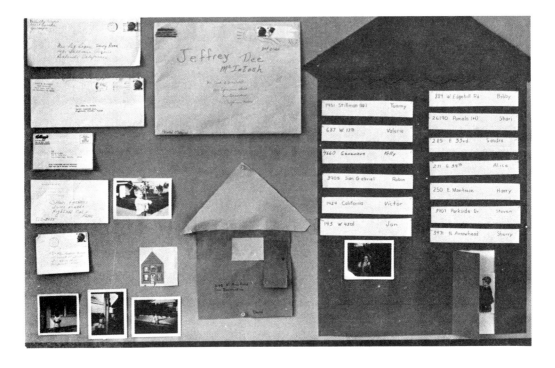

addresses. Give each child a cardboard label with his address on it and let each one take a turn pinning his own address to the house. Repeat the activity daily until each child can select his own address from a box of labels.

Related Activities Have each child make a paper house from precut pieces—body, roof, windows, door. Cut the roofs from papers of various textures (wallpaper samples are good for this). If the child knows his address, write it on his paper house and send the house home with him. For the child who has not learned his address, write a note on the house saying, "Please help me learn my address."

• With the younger or immature child, concentrate on helping him learn the name of his street and the color of his house. In emergencies, most children can recognize their own homes once they are on the right street.

• Draw a large make-believe map of the city and locate each child's house on the map. Have each child draw or paste a cutout house in his "location." Play a delivery game. Today each house will get a new tree. The child who can remember the address of his house may paste a cutout tree somewhere on his lot. Fences can be built, TV antennas installed, groceries delivered. The possibilities are almost limitless. Repeat the activity about once a month throughout the school year.

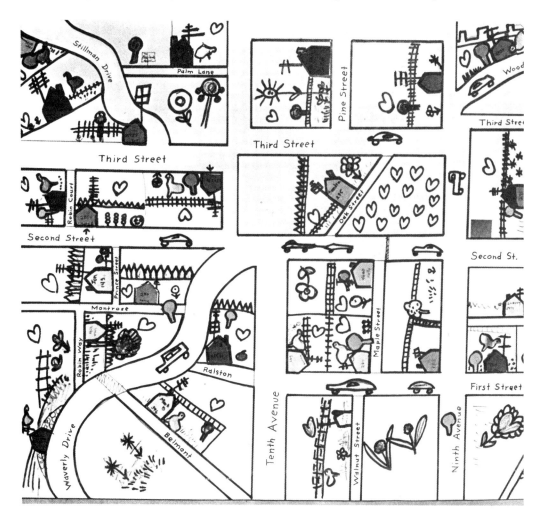

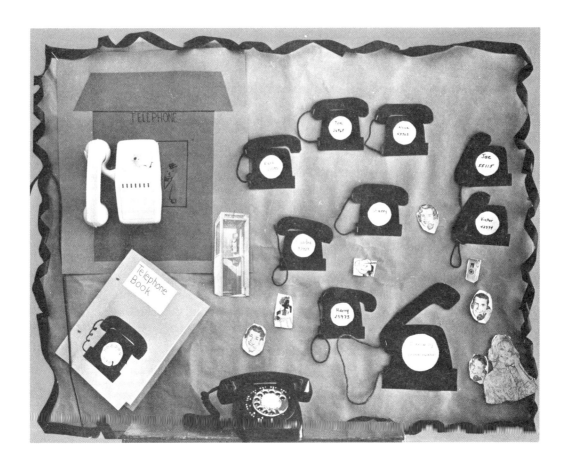

TELEPHONE NUMBERS

Give each child a telephone cut from black construction paper (or colored paper, if you wish). Write the child's phone number on a white paper disc pasted to the phone dial, then pin the phones on a bulletin board display. When a child learns his own phone number and can locate his phone on the board, he may use it to make "calls."

Related Activities A large cardboard shipping carton can become a corner telephone booth. Let the class decorate it (tempera paint mixed with canned milk produces a hard, durable finish). You might want to hang a toy wall phone on the wall of the booth so the children can practice calling "home." Some children may also want to learn the telephone numbers of their closest friends.

• Contact the public relations department of your local phone company and ask to borrow educational films for young children on proper telephone use. Let each child practice what he has observed by using the class phone booth. Then as a special treat, let him call home from a school phone. As an incentive to those who haven't learned their phone numbers, make the home call a motivation for learning.

• Compile a class phone book and hang it on the phone booth. Children enjoy finding their own phone numbers in the book, and some will use it to learn the numbers of their friends.

SELF-CONCEPT

The Birthday Board

A large paper cutout cake, covered with colored paper decorations (let children do the decorating) awaits the candles of the birthday child. On his birthday each child can select the color and size of candles he wants for the cake. Older children may wish to make colored paper cutout gift boxes, decorate them, and add them to the display.

    Related Activities If you are in a community where families are likely to have photographic records of their children, send a note home about ten days before a child's birthday asking for several pictures of the child at different ages. Feature the "birthday child" on a special bulletin board.

• The child whose birthday falls in a vacation period shouldn't be left out of the ongoing excitement. Chart the "in school" birthdays and then distribute the others evenly in between.

- Let children make birthday cards for one another. Their contributions can be strung on yarn and hung on the walls for decoration. After his birthday has been celebrated, the child can take the collection home and share it with his family.

- Make a large giraffe out of orange velour paper and decorate him with black spots. Children will enjoy petting his fury coat. Use the neck of the giraffe for a growth chart and measure each child at regular intervals. Let children use rulers to measure how much they have grown. If drawing a giraffe is beyond your artistic aspirations, then use a simpler object such as a tree trunk or a ladder.

Smile, Smile, Smile

Prepare a display board for a collage by cutting a hole in the board and taping a mirror on its back to cover the hole. Supply the class with old magazines and catalogs and have them cut out all the smiling faces they can find and paste them onto the board. Encourage the child to study his own face and think about his expressions as he observes them in the mirror. This is an important aspect of developing a positive self-concept. A full length mirror is an excellent addition to a classroom.

This display is helpful in discussing emotional responses and how they are revealed through facial expressions. They are pleasing (and often amusing) to touch as well as look at. Provide a container of shapes (circles, triangles, arcs) and yarn for the child to use in creating other facial expressions.

Something Quiet

This, too, can be a child-created display. Use old magazines and catalogs and have children cut appropriate pictures from them. Give them as few directions as possible so their imaginations will be free and they can make their choices on a child's level.

- Discuss "quiet." Ask: "What is the quietest thing you can think of?" "How do you feel when you think of something quiet?" Then have pupils show, through facial expressions, how they feel about something quiet. Ask them to "move like something quiet."

- Vary the board by occasionally covering it with a sheet of heavy blue plastic to create a twilight mood. Children may wish to add a moon and stars to the twilight scene. Talk about things that you see, hear, and do in the evening hours.

Night and Day

Discuss differences between nighttime and daytime. What things do you think of when you think of daytime? Nighttime? How do things look in daylight? In moonlight? As a basis for discussions and activities, create a daytime/nighttime bulletin board. Use cloth for the background (dark blue for night and light blue for day). Add the other elements (darker colors for night and lighter shades of the same colors for day). Glitter can be glued to the nighttime side as stars, or children may wish to use stick-on stars.

To extend the idea of light and dark, night and day, this bulletin board display shows supplementary lighting for nighttime use and safety. The four pictures are based on cutouts from magazines. The globe on the streetlight and headlights on the car were accentuated by yellow felt, and cotton was pulled into whispy strands to create the feeling of light rays.

Related Activities Make a night and day peep show from a shoe box. Cut a hole in each end of the box, then divide the box in the center with a large piece of cardboard. Place a small tree (break off a portion of a woody bush or use a plastic one) on either side of the divider. Cut an opening in the top of each half of the lid to provide a light source. Cover one half with two layers of yellow cellophane or tissue paper and cover the other opening with two layers of blue. Have the children describe what they see as they peer through each end of the box.

SHADOWS

This display illustrates the power of a simple message. Questions to be explored include:

> What is a shadow?
>
> Where does it come from?
>
> Why does it go away sometimes?
>
> Is it always in the same place?
>
> What else can make shadows besides the sun?

To make this display, cut out two figures of a child, one from white paper and one from black. Paste the figures on the board as shown. Add a shining sun to complete the display.

Related Activities Use a flashlight to create shadows. Show children how to make shadow pictures on the wall using a flashlight as a light source. Once pupils have an understanding of the simple front-lighted shadow show, you can construct a shadow theater. String a wire across the room and hang a sheet over it. Place strong lighting behind it, and have your actors perform between the lights and the sheet. Make certain that the rest of the room is fairly dark.

TIME

Learning cannot be an isolated experience. It must be coordinated with all the activities of a child in order to be meaningful. Displays must be selected carefully to satisfy the changing needs and interests of the child.

Paper Plate Clock

The child needs and wants to know how to tell time. He wants to know when to tune in his favorite TV shows, when to leave for school, how long he can stay at a friend's house.

- Make a paper plate clock with hands that move. Move the hands of the clock to match the hands on the wall clock to show passage of time from one activity to another. Let pupils move the hands and discuss telling time from a clock.

  Related Activities Have pupils make their own paper plate clocks using cardboard hands, a brass fastener, and a paper plate. You will have to make the numerals for the younger ones. Use these clocks in a variety of time-telling activities.

The Television Schedule

- Television is a great time medium. Days, hours, minutes are important to television and through it the child often comes to his first real understandings of time.

- Create a cardboard box TV set from a shallow carton. Cut a large opening for the screen, then paint the set with tempera mixed with canned milk. Using nuts and bolts, attach knobs made from spools (washers will keep the bolts from pulling out). Tape a sheet of clear plastic on the inside of the opening.

  Related Activities Schedule activities for different times during the day and attach the schedule to the set.

- Use the box for a variety of games. Children can report on school events, family vacations, the weather, and coming events. Give them opportunities to think of ways to use the TV set for other classroom activities.

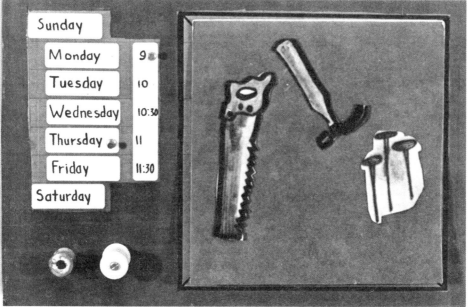

Calendars

Learning cannot be an isolated experience. It must be coordinated with all his activities for it to be meaningful to a child. I like to use one-week calendars with young children.

- Make the calendar page large enough to hold a child's illustrations or whole pages from magazines. Some days will require more than one illustration.
- Make the calendar page colorful and make it fun. Use humor, cartoons, and jokes whenever possible.

- Keep it simple. A child's name on a cake can mark a birthday. A field trip can be represented by a single picture of one of the many things to be seen. Choose a significant object to represent a classroom activity.

- Watch for changes around you. Notice when the flowers start to blossom and mark the event on the calendar. Listen to the child's conversations. The arrival of a new litter of kittens is of great importance to all. Note it with an appropriate picture. Build up a file of "situation" pictures cut from magazines so that you have quick access to pictures to mark special events.

- Take care to select harmonizing colors and add decorations from time to time. If it's worth noting on the calendar, it's worth the time to make it appealing.

- Remember, when you're small and growing fast, events are momentous and changes are very important.

SEASONS

This chart gives children another way to measure time. By starting the dial at the appropriate point in time and advancing it a little each week, the child begins to develop another understanding of the passage of time.

Weather

This chart is used in conjunction with the seasons chart. We used two dials to help the child understand that weather comes in various combinations. The sections represent: hot; very, very hot; warm but not sunny (between the two suns); white clouds; storm clouds; foggy or smoggy (same section); wind; rain; snow; cold . (icicles).

- To make this display, use the same method as for the seasons chart. Cut ten pie shaped wedges and, by overlapping, fit them into a circular pattern. *Variation*: Instead of drawing, I have made a similar display using weather scenes cut from illustrated magazines.

HELPER CHARTS _____

Having a Helper Chart provides a check for the teacher in fair and equal assignment of tasks (which children find an important form of recognition). The child responds positively to finding his name displayed on the chart, even on those days when he is not assigned to any classroom task.

- This chart has been designed with the following in mind:

  The meaningful use of symbols

  Exercises in visual perception as the child follows the rubber bands from names to tasks

  Different ways of writing names

  Preventing the aggressive child from overpowering his shyer classmates

- The chart can be changed to combine additional teaching. For example, shapes and colors can be used as clues. A child has a red triangle as his symbol, so he looks on the chart for the task that has a red triangle attached to it. Later on, letter forms or numerals can be used.

32

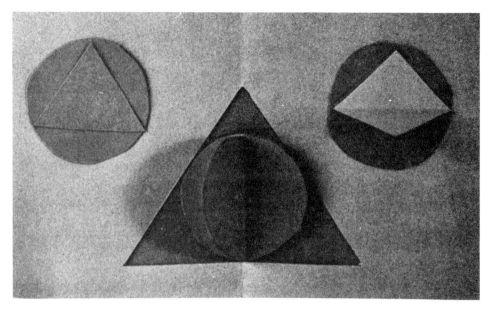

SHAPES

A basic understanding of shape recognition and identification is vital to the young child's success in early academic activities. Interesting and involving bulletin boards can be developed to help the child gain competence in recognizing shapes, spatial relationships, proportions, and related concepts.

- Some ideas that can be explored include:

    Fitting a square inside a circle

    Half a square is a triangle

    A diamond can be (but doesn't have to be) a square standing on its nose

    Some rectangles, when folded in half, make two squares

- Give the child shapes to manipulate and fold. Let him experiment (you may wish to give a few directions at first) and discuss the results of their experiments.

- Let each child make designs: same size and shape, different colors; same shape and color, different sizes; same size and color, different shapes; same size, different colors and shapes. Discuss his designs with him and make a display of the finished work.

- Three-dimensional displays and manipulative devices are also of great value. Wooden or plastic blocks or other objects can create a nearby interest center to enhance the meaning of the display. Discuss the blocks, compare them, arrange them in designs. Have the children talk about what they observe and experience.

STREET SCENE

- To capitalize on the ideas already explored in the previous activities, we discussed many types of products that can be bought. We then made a street mural and shopping center. The stores were cut from fadeless art paper in colors the children chose. Ordinary construction paper will work equally well, but if exposed to light for any length of time it will lose most of its color.

- Once the stores were complete, we talked about them and their functions. Then I drew an item in the window of one and encouraged children to add items of their own. The mural grew as merchandise, shoppers, automobiles, and so on were added by the children. The mural could be easily stored and revived periodically as interests dictated.

CATEGORIZING

These three bulletin board displays offer experiences in sequencing.

Bread

> First the farmer sows his seed (glue real seeds onto the display)
> Rain makes the seeds grow
> So does the sunlight
> The ripe wheat is ready to harvest

Study these drawings and see how simple it is to create a bulletin board. Draw a farmer, or cut an illustration from a book or magazine. Use him as the focal point of your drawings. Keep your drawings simple.

Eggs

This picture sequence needs no further explanation. If the chicken is beyond your artistic talents, cut one from a coloring book or old picture book.

Milk

This sequence is simple enough for the very youngest child to comprehend. The two cows in the upper portion of the display are easily taken off the board and handled by the child. In setting up the board, use a piece of heavy green construction paper and fold it up on the bottom to form a pocket-chart type insert.

• Dairy products can be added to the display one at a time as they are discussed in class.

THE RESTAURANT

The food concept can be further explored through a restaurant. Set up a table with paper plates that have magazine ad cutout pictures of food pasted onto them. The children may enjoy playing restaurant, ordering and serving special meals. Older groups may want to set prices for different items and use play money for paying bills.

Related Activities   As a backdrop for dramatic play and role-playing, portable displays, like the one pictured here, can be made. You need no special art talents. I used the following steps in creating a restaurant play area:

A refrigerator carton (appliance stores are usually glad to have them hauled away) was opened lengthwise and painted. I used blue tempera mixed with canned milk (for a more permanent surface). It took the children two days to complete the painting of the background.

On the third day, space for the floor was marked off and several children painted that area black. (It was necessary for me to outline the design with chalk.) To get the perspective correct, I cut out several pictures of kitchens from women's magazines and used them as models.

Corrugated display paper was then cut to form the serving counters. In the one pictured here, pink paper was used.

The figures were made by folding pieces of lightweight poster board in half and cutting them out as you would cut paper dolls. The arms were added separately and paper fasteners made them moveable. Children take great delight in shaking hands with the figures, putting the figures in new and interesting position, and so on.

I used strips of masking tape and scraps of patterned cloth to add finishing touches to the display.

Paper plates are pinned on with straight pins and can be changed from time to time. In the photograph, the "food" is formed by wads of colored tissue. We decided that they represented spinach, hamburger, and fruit. A sponge makes a sandwich and thin sponges make good slices of bread. We have also used them as pieces of cake.

The paper plates in the picture are a few from an assortment of about fifty different ones which have been prepared by children. One to three small tables are usually set up in front of the display. Some of the plates are displayed, and from the displays the customer can select his menu. We usually have a waitress or waiter and a cashier.

Other Uses for Backdrops

Similar backgrounds can be created for playing bank, postoffice, supermarket, and doctor or dentist. The boards can be folded and stored when not in use. If you are short on space, you can paint backdrops on both sides of your cartons, thus getting two for the space of one.

HOLIDAY MURALS

Sometimes a mural makes a good holiday project in which children and teacher cooperate. This provides a good opportunity for children to learn to work together on a cooperative project. This mural was painted on a brown wrapping paper background. The turkeys were drawn by the teacher and cut out by children, who also pasted on paper strips as "feathers."

Spring

Another mural that can be used with five- and six-year-olds is a spring scene. By this time of year, children have had enough experience in mural making to work as an effective team, and their interests have developed sufficiently to carry plans and ideas across a several week span. The mural in this illustration was prepared in the following way:

> Large sheets of paper were spread out on the floor. Over a period of about three days the entire background was covered with "sky" (light blue tempera paint). We used sponges to apply the paint.

> Trees were then added (with younger groups, the teacher may have to handle this aspect of the mural) using dark brown paint.

> Green tissue paper leaves were then added to the trees (the mural is still on the floor).

> The mural was then fastened to a long, low bulletin board (placement is crucial as the children still have lots of work to do on it).

> A long strip of wrapping paper was then painted various shades of green and cut into 6"–8" strips and pasted along the bottom of the mural to represent grass.

> During the following weeks, small groups of children worked with the teacher to add spring "things" to the mural: butterflies, flowers, birds, clouds.

• The mural is a great example of teamwork and cooperation and gives the child a real sense of identity with the group because everyone has an important role in its creation.

- The bugs were made out of half sections of cardboard egg cartons. Each child was free to do whatever he pleased with his creations—add colors, pipe cleaner appendages, tissue paper wings, and miscellaneous decorations.

- The butterflies are rectangular shapes of tissue paper caught in the middle with pipe cleaners and squeezed to form the butterfly shapes. Wing decorations were added with colored tempera paint.

- No patterns were used to create the flowers. Miscellaneous sizes of paper squares and circles were supplied and the children experimented with different combinations and layers. The creations were finished off with green pipe-cleaner stems.

How Do the Flowers Grow?

As the mural was being constructed, we were busy planting seeds in indoor planters. This diagram of how flowers grow further expanded the learning experiences. Most important, there were real seeds to touch and real plants to water and observe daily. The activity culminated with a transplanting ceremony in a nearby outdoor garden.

POLLIWOG POND

We were studying water creatures and one day, following a story session about frogs and polliwogs, a child asked for a scissors, cut out a shape she had drawn, and said, "It's a polliwog."

- The teacher then created a pond from blue construction paper with a beach of brown construction paper. The child was then asked to put her polliwog in the pond. Soon two frogs and a turtle were added by other children. As the study unit progressed, other children made their own contributions to the display board. Each new addition was the subject for discussion and questioning.

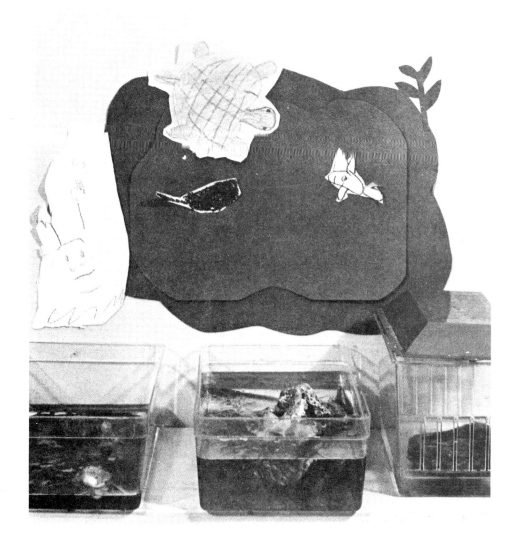

SILKWORMS

Spring brings silkworms as our classroom supply of eggs hatch into active, wiggly, puffy white silkworms. Their growth and changes come very fast; from egg through worm, cocoon, and finally to moth, takes a very few weeks, a short enough period for a small child to observe the changes and relate them to earlier stages.

Related Activities   Make large model silkworms from white styrofoam egg boxes by cutting the bottom of the box lengthwise. Each strip (two to a carton) forms the body of the model silkworm. Add pipe-cleaner feelers, then mount the worms on a bulletin board background of mulberry branches and leaves.

- One morning when the children arrive, they find that some of the paper leaves have been chewed. On another morning they find that one silkworm has spun a cocoon (white yarn). (After a seemingly endless winding job, I discovered that a pad of tissue paper around the egg carton "worm" makes the task much more bearable.)

- Later, real silkworm cocoons (empty) are added to the display (see #3 in the photograph). Later we added a top and bottom view of two dead moths (see #4) in a see-through plastic box. Higher up, and out of the reach of children, is a moth. Next to the jar of real live silkworms is a cage (a plastic bleach bottle and wire screening) ready to receive the moths as they appear. Most are turned loose in the mulberry trees and a few are kept to provide eggs for next year's exhibit.

BUS TRIPS

Bus trips and excursions are always exciting experiences for the children. We usually introduce them with these bus displays. The front view of the bus was cut from gummed colored paper. The picture of the driver and the passengers and the headlights were pasted onto the colored paper. The wheels are from a broken toy car. They poke through slits cut into the mounting board. They are attached in back with Scotch tape. The wheels actually turn, which makes the display even more attractive to the children. The two side views of buses are also made from gummed colored paper pasted onto a cardboard background. The wheels are made from discarded 8mm movie film spools.